WOODPECKERS

BACKYARD BIRDS

Lynn Stone

The Rourke Corporation, Inc.
Vero Beach, Florida 32964

PHOTO CREDITS
© Tom Vezo: cover, pages 8, 10; © Lynn M. Stone: pages 4, 12, 15, 18, title page; © Tom Ulrich: pages 7, 13; © Marie Read: page 21; page 17 courtesy of Aspects, Inc. Warren, RI

COVER ART:
James Spence

EDITORIAL SERVICES:
Penworthy Learning Systems

Library of Congress Cataloging-in-Publication Data

Stone, Lynn M.
  Woodpeckers / by Lynn M. Stone.
    p. cm. — (Backyard birds)
  Includes index
  Summary: Describes the physical characteristics, habitats, and behavior of different kinds of woodpeckers, including the flicker, gila woodpecker, and red-bellied woodpecker.
  ISBN 0-86593-470-3
  1. Woodpeckers—Juvenile literature. [1. Woodpeckers.] I. Title II. Series.
Stone, Lynn M. Backyard birds.
QL696.P56S76 1998
598.7'2—dc21   98–11209
                                                              CIP
                                                              AC

Printed in the USA

TABLE OF CONTENTS

WOODPECKERS

Woodpeckers are drummers with feathers. With their sharp beaks, woodpeckers hammer at tree trunks. They make loud *rat-a-tat-tat* sounds.

The noise does not even give the woodpecker a headache, though. A woodpecker's head has muscles that cushion the blows.

A woodpecker hammers bark and wood to make holes in trees. The bird finds food in some holes. In other larger holes, it makes its nest.

Woodpeckers cling to tree trunks, which they hammer for food and nest holes.

WHAT WOODPECKERS LOOK LIKE

Most woodpeckers are handsome birds, black-and-white with red trim. They have sharp beaks and stiff tail feathers. Those tail feathers help a woodpecker balance on a tree trunk.

The North American **species** (SPEE sheez), or kinds, of woodpeckers may be small or large. The little downy woodpecker is the size of a large sparrow. The pileated (PYE lee AY tid) woodpecker is crow size!

The largest North American woodpeckers, the ivory-billed and the imperial, are probably **extinct** (ex STINGKT)—gone forever.

Many kinds of woodpeckers, such as this red-bellied, have rows of black and white feathers on their back.

WHERE WOODPECKERS LIVE

Most kinds of woodpeckers live in or near forests or open woodlots. They stay on the trunks or branches of trees.

The flicker is not like most woodpeckers. It likes to eat ants, and it often feeds on the ground.

The gila woodpecker is unusual, too. It lives in giant saguaro cactus instead of trees.

Woodpeckers live in the wooded parts of Mexico, Canada, and the United States. They also live in South America, Europe, Asia, and Africa.

This flicker visits a beach to look for ants in the sand.

THE WOODPECKER FAMILY

Scientists know over 200 species of woodpeckers. Twenty-one species live in the United States and Canada.

Some North American woodpeckers are known as flickers or sapsuckers. In other countries birds called piculets, wrynecks, flamebacks, and yellownapes are part of the woodpecker family.

Woodpeckers of all kinds have long, sharp tongues. The tongues can reach into tree holes or under bark to find insects.

The yellow-bellied sapsucker hammers holes that let tree sap ooze out.

This red-headed woodpecker has chipped out a nest hole in a dead oak tree.

A downy woodpecker brings a meal of plump insects to its babies.

WOODPECKERS IN THE BACKYARD

Your backyard need not be a forest to have woodpeckers in it. Many woodpeckers like to visit trees that are in open places. They especially like dead trees.

Some species, such as downy, hairy, and red-headed woodpeckers, will even move into backyard nesting boxes. The box, though, needs to be covered with bark. Then it looks like part of a real tree.

The flicker, Alabama's state bird, likes yards where it can find ants.

A pileated woodpecker used this dead palm tree for a nest.

BACKYARD FOOD FOR WOODPECKERS

Woodpeckers eat insects most of the year. In winter they eat other goodies at **feeding stations** (FEE ding STAY shunz).

Most woodpeckers eat **suet** (SOO it). Suet is hardened animal fat. Flickers like peanut butter.

Red-bellied woodpeckers like orange slices and cracked corn. Nutmeats are a favorite food of red-bellied and red-headed woodpeckers. Red-headed woodpeckers also like sunflower seeds.

A red-bellied woodpecker shares a seed feeder with a cardinal.

WOODPECKER HABITS

Woodpeckers do not often perch, or sit, on branches. Instead, they cling upright to the trunks.

Tree trunks are a woodpecker's picnic table. A woodpecker's beak cuts away bark and wood chips. Then the bird's long, sticky tongue can grab insects that were hidden.

For a woodpecker, the sapsucker has an unusual diet. It eats **sap** (SAP) that oozes from the holes it hammers.

Sap drips from holes that a sapsucker drilled into this sugar maple.

WOODPECKER NESTS

Woodpeckers, like bluebirds and wood ducks, are **cavity** (KAV eh tee) nesters. A cavity in your tooth is a small hole. Most woodpeckers make a cavity, or hole, in a tree for their nests. The gila woodpecker hammers its nest hole in a giant cactus. Inside the cavity, a woodpecker lines the bottom with wood chips.

Hammering out a nest hole is a job that takes several days. Each year the woodpeckers make a new nest. Old woodpecker nest holes are used by other animals.

Young flickers look out at the big, new world beyond their nest hole.

BABY WOODPECKERS

Woodpeckers usually lay three to five eggs. The number depends upon the kind of woodpecker. All woodpecker eggs are white.

After they hatch, baby woodpeckers grow up in the nest hole. The adult woodpeckers bring food to them.

Baby downy woodpeckers live in the nest for three weeks before they can fly. Pileated babies take nearly a month to grow up.

Glossary

cavity (KAV eh tee) — a hole

extinct (ex STINGKT) — gone forever, as in the disappearance of an entire species of animal or plant

feeding station (FEE ding STAY shun) — a place where people put food for birds; a birdfeeder

sap (SAP) — a sticky, syrup-like liquid in trees

species (SPEE sheez) — within a group of closely related animals, one certain kind, such as a *red-headed* woodpecker

suet (SOO it) — hardened animal fat

INDEX

FURTHER READING:

Find out more about Backyard Birds with these helpful books and information sites:

• Burnie, David. *Bird*. Knopf, 1988
• Cooper, Jason. *Birds, the Rourke Guide to State Symbols*. Rourke, 1997
• Mahnken, Jan. *The Backyard Bird-Lover's Guide*. Storey Communications, 1996
• Parsons, Alexandra. *Amazing Birds*. Knopf, 1990
• *Field Guide to the Birds of North America*. National Geographic, 1983
• Cornell Laboratory of Ornithology online at http://birdsource.cornell.edu
• National Audubon Society online at www.audubon.org